the witch bag

To Lugh and Ruari,
my beloved family

We fall asleep
with one hand under our head
and with the other in a mound of planets

– Zbigniew Herbert

...We who are still alive, living in the often
fibrillating heartland of a senescent capitalism –
can we do more than reflect the decay around
and within us? Can we do more than sing our
sad and bitter songs of disillusion and defeat?

– R. D. Laing, *The Politics of Experience*

sarah corbett
the witch bag

seren

Seren is the book imprint of
Poetry Wales Press Ltd
Nolton Street, Bridgend, Wales
www.seren-books.com

ISBN 1-85411-322-4

A CIP record for this title is available from
the British Library

The publisher works with the financial assistance of the
Arts Council of Wales

Cover image: *Qualia* (detail), 2001 by Mary Husted
Photograph: Dave Brook

Printed in Palatino by
Bell & Bain Ltd, Glasgow

Contents

The Witch Bag

Remember me. I am the woman
who shook her fisted nipples
at the moon,
bearing down the dark streets
that could not take her.

My face broke in two
as I ate its bright cheek,
my hands sudden as marshlight
held before me
into the dark nights that followed.

I am the woman who flew
not only in her dreams,
but remembered the spell as she woke
and hunted sighs like ticks,
dipping and turning as she went.

That woman, weightless thing,
thin as pond moss,
blacker than the pond's black belly.
She hooks its clammy limbs around her own
and sucks the water into herself.

That woman, without a world,
who goes hopping with one boot
between twilights,
a bagful of grave treasures
lost and lost again –

mask of hair, milk tooth,
heel-bone, blood-purse, name.

The Wheel

She has come back, my dead child,
inevitable as winter. Here she is, still
against a cold bright window, her hands

folded in her lap. She never cried,
she never tightened her small fist on my finger;
I have killed her over and over

with my heart's black stone. However hard
I prise her from my bone she stays,
the wheel that binds me to this fact

of returning. My body makes destruction
in the circuit of its blood; it is a well
left to sing through its mask of weeds

an insistent and purposeful madness.
I lower myself into its green and stinking hole.
I may or may not draw back water.

My Three Dead Daughters

1. Green Rose

First, I was tenderly young.
Second, I believed myself empty of sex.
So when I sickened, ballooned,
I thought it was fear breaking
out of its egg at last.

Your father kicked down the door,
dragged me by the hair
and raped me in the cold backyard.
How was I to know of your heat
in that bitter pod inside?

When, at twelve weeks, I heard
of your presence, your Thumbelina
arms, legs, spine perfecting
in the walnut shell of my womb,
the black earth bloomed.

OK, I engineered your death,
but woke after wanting you back,
searched all the rubbish bins
in all the backyards from here to Liverpool,
broke my teeth at the clinic walls.

You are my daughter of the green rose,
you demand water daily. You root,
put out leaves to catch my rain.
Your closed buds never flower
but hold tight the colour of my crime.

2. Half-Moon Baby

I wanted you, oh yes. There was great passion
at your making. I knew you the moment
you set your delicate silvery foot
in the tracery of my veins. My blood buzzed
and gathered like gossips to make your bed.

I even made a garden for you from the greenest
scraps of my past: the primrose patch
where you bent your face to the clusters of light,
dampening your cotton dress on the moss
under the dark of the wishing oak.

I named you many times – Griselda, Daphne,
Rosalind – considered the colours of your hair,
how they would turn with the years,
forgot I would not keep you past one moon and one half,
and forgetting, took the bright pill.

3. Crow Girl

So you came to avenge your sisters.
First you were a spider wrapping your cords
around my heart to wrench out the feeling.
Then you put your black wire legs
into feather stockings, grew a black beak
to crack the carefully pieced mosaic of my soul.

You did not leave, but flew to the branches
of a tree where it was always winter,
its naked canopy burnt into a flayed sky.
Here, you became a girl in a muddied skin
and from your gold rimmed eyes kept look out
for your lost sisters, your lost mother.

Black Crow Woman

Hear me singing.
My songs are crueller than mountain songs
trapped in their cold snows.

I have a shadow so deep
it would eat you, or worry your sleep
to madness so that you would eat

your own children to be free of me.

The hour never turns that I do not know
how it lays its weight on babies
until they cannot breathe

and must bleed out their hearts from little holes,
how it calls the birds to fall from the air
to feed the starving pavements

and chokes every skyline with its black hands.

Draw my deaths from me, one by one.
My bones are a graveyard of bones
where the dead pile their grievances.

They circle as the crows circle the tired day,
calling and calling for the night to relieve them.

I will show you what a dark word love is,

how generous it is to suffer,
laying your body as a bridge
for others to pass into morning.

Little Bitch

Poems fall from her as rain
dirty rain on a polluted city,
rain that stains your skirt,
laces its soot in your hair,
rain that blackens your blood;

water become food it's so thick,
food for your skin, a protective
scum, river mud caked
and drying on a sow's back,
cracking to dust in the sun.

This is how she is: coated
in the claggy sods of words,
eyes bruised to their lips
with all the hurt, throat grimed,
hands conspiratorial with dirt.

Down like this she's blathery,
drunk on her own sugars,
bitching out her loves to burst,
a drain shedding debris. Under pressure
she takes handfuls of herself, throws.

Leda and Me

There is a lightness in me
and I am thinking of Leda,
how she might have felt after the swan,
how another being entering you must change you,
how surely you take on something of them.

I like to believe she dreamt
of floating on lakes under the moon,
sweeping heavily through the air
lifted by warm currents under wings,
that weeks after she noticed tiny transparent follicles
sprouting from her arms and chest
until she was spilling feathers wherever she went.

I send a finger under the sleeve of my jumper,
stroke the sleek insides of my elbows
and wrists, where the blue veins stand out
amidst their plumage
like heroines in fifties horror films
swooning and pouting into the arms of men.

Dream

A dream gave me a gift:
a mouse or a small bird
with wings of tarnished silver
raised to an armoured point.

It sat on my shoulder,
claws piercing the skin
and drawing six red beads
that rolled into my lap.

It turned a mechanical dance
clanking its slatted feathers,
dropped in my hand a glass egg
that became a blue eye,

now my eye as I crank
the machinery of my wings,
heave the ton of my belly
above a sleeping city.

Meeting

I come for a face
to hold myself to,
as if meeting my other
could make two things add up.

But she reflects nothing,
not even light travels past her,
only how surprised
my own eyes are in the mirror.

She tells me her dream –
a field of dead horses,
clambering over their swollen bellies,
frantic for a child's hand –

how it comes each month
with her blood's force,
keeps coming, as her body shifts
beyond its tense.

This is our pain:
silence held like a gun.
Raising her hand to mine
her wrist is scored with it.

She is rain on metal,
persistent, corrosive,
sand moving, shaping
what she moves against.

I cannot hold out,
her mouth cuts despite
its softness, like wings in glass
because of butterflies.

Gift

You rise into my hands: horse,
water gathering below ground,
a muscular swell,
like the blood tide.

Between us the spine's ghost
shudders its spidery tail
and across the moor
the spooked herd gallops.

Oh, the wind is a wide smile,
the land is light, light
and travels within us;
as we pass the trees burn.

We obey breath, touch, earth.
When again the eagle
crosses our path, we enter
the slow amber of its flight.

The Kitchen God

1

When you first came we had fat queen olives
Marinated in herbed oil with every dish,
Raw coriander sharpening the rich
Soups and curries, cumin speckled breads, cloves,
Their lusty oil seeping into our clothes
From the skin; garlic by the bulb, radish,
Chilli sliced and dangerous to the touch;
Nutmeg wines, ginger teas, cinnamon toast.

You made the whole kitchen yours. Food smelted
You, your flesh and hair tinctured, scented in spice,
Your whole body one hot place to be rubbed,
Peeled, primed for the palate, a flavour held
A long time on the tongue, requiring ice
In the mouth to steady your taster's pulse.

2

You brought your fire cooking, translating wood
Gathered at first light: coax, stoke, blow, crackle
Of kindling under the flame, the bubble,
Ooze of sap as a branch burns into good-
Ness, raw warmth on faces, the fire's given food.
Remember that big black-bottomed kettle,
The first pot of the day's tea set to boil,
Chappatis, finger made, carob sweet, grilled?

Then the others coming, couples sleeping
At the fire warmed awake, a lone child drawn
By a smoke promise drifting through the trees;
And me now, scenting breakfast simmering
Through the house, nudged from sleep,
                                        a dream that haunts
All morning like the sharp bloom of brewed leaves.

3

I taught you to make bread. I said, patience,
My love, is the key. Remember the hash
Cookies burnt sugar bitter, boot-black?
(We had them with tea. They brought visions).
For those three hours we agreed silence.
By gesture I showed you: my body, hands,
Touch-knowing all over again the craft
Of dough, its textured weight held until learnt.

Moist warm, rising is the best. Watch now
For the elastic flesh to swell. Proving
In darkness under a damp cloth, it grew
Towards the next thump of muscle. Its brown
And woody smell was coming from your skin.
You grew, initiated; love followed.

4

I thought perhaps you were a sugared fruit
Left long in the sun, those tangy crystals
Surfacing through your flesh to the skin (full,
Washed deep in its perfume). I bit into
The promise and prophecy this flush suit
Like harvest brings, found a nest of wasps tails
That caught and stung my tongue. My quick
                                        mouth swelled
At the poison, a warning I refused.

But you are plentiful, always ready
To fall from your branch, roll into my hands.
You give up your surface to the pared white
Rawness beneath, my edged fingers heavy
With rapacious love. I forget, burr-blind
In your fragrance, the waiting, hoarded blight.

5

Food-Faggot, Bread-Thief, Hog's-Dinner, Cuckoo,
Sauce-Stealer, Pan-Taster, the lion's proof
Of majesty picking clean to the hoof
What I've caught, slain, offered up to you,
Tracking delicacies all afternoon;
The last sliver in my dish that soothes
Your appetite fed to your waiting mouth:
Slippery fingers against a sharp tooth.

Something must give, I'm running on empty:
Slim-line, fasted as you soften, fill out.
What was that music you first brought to mind?
L'Apres Midi D'Un Faun. Debussy
Should see you now: A Falstaff, or Faust,
Restless for the hunger in flesh you find.

6

Darling, I know this craving, loathed desire.
We could name it Love, draw the parallel
Of infatuation and disgust, smell
Of stale sex that awakes you, stokes your fire
From the ashes until you're asking for more.
Yet in waking, the appetite repels
The body from its excesses. And still
You cram a skin-full, load your flesh, perspire.

However, let us balance our dining
With our fucking, crumb the sheets with biscuit
Aperitifs; utilise the kitchen,
Its opportunities for invention,
A tray at the bedside with titbits
Shared between meals to keep the body keen.

7

Food is your element, our days portioned
Between servings, what waits cool in cupboards,
Jars, bottles, greased wrappings, shelves stacked
                                        to hoard
Half-forgotten flavours lying unnamed
In reclaimed honey pots, their pure, ancient
Power a subtle healing packed, known, stored
In the uncracked grain. By rule, you make more
Than needed; supper is always eaten.

You cook while I write, bring cups of dark herb,
Crisp brown toast. Do you remember
When I was pregnant? I loved that red spiced
Soup with lentils, a glob of yoghurt stirred
In, your unleavened bread, salt and pepper
Tarting the dough, dipped and sucked. So, so nice.

8

A feast! Who grew the spinach that graces
The salad? You did. Who cultured and tamed
Tomatoes all summer to plush inflamed
Fruit we now hold and admire, faces
Sun-flushed as their heavy skins? Traces
Of their flavour linger long. We shall name
Them for you: Ruari – Red Faced One – shame
Of sweetness and desire, wantonness....

Satisfied, plump and puffed, drowsy on cheap
Wine, we fill the bed, spill over towards
Dreams, sighs, giggles, tomorrow's half-formed
                                        thoughts.
Our bellies, loved one, meet even in sleep,
Pressed close as the pea-green halves of a pod,
Mine, seeded again, growing towards yours.

Feast

Five blue swans you brought me,
patterned finely as porcelain,
carved, you said, from regret,
sorrow, grief, despair; except the last
being a thing lost, a shadow.

They stood on your wrists,
your shoulders, the fifth paddled
your back, flourished lapis wings,
curled the ess of their necks:
your aura, your sex, your language.

Your heart was a plume, oiled
and resistant. Showing me this,
sadness silvered your cheeks,
a river of pearls in your hands
where the birds fed delicately.

You cut off their heads,
hung them to dry where they danced
in the wind – five abandoned dresses –
served their breasts with jewels
dug from their throats.

You fattened with pride as I feasted,
my fingers claggy with juice,
my mouth huge with desire.
When I had finished I spat out pearls,
wove the bones in my hair.

Fiesta

We got drunk, that was the first thing. We mixed
Our spirits, and in a strange city too.
I knew it was dangerous, after shoot-
Ings. Besides, we were outsiders, un-tricked
By the carnival revellers, the twist
Of costume into uniform, the blue
And white too obvious a mark of who
Belonged, who could only watch and be watched.

Later, the row blew. We were losing track
Of the streets. They took us ever outwards,
Each corner hustled danger, grew darker.
Take me back, I pleaded, *take me back, back.*
Our room was crowded with heat, parade drums,
A woman's screaming from the corridor.

Heron

Sighting us, it lifted
from the shallow river bed,
turned to the cold wind coming east.

A birth, I said, *a birth*,
and hugged the flat deceiving belly.
You took my hand.

Only against the brown land
could we mark its detail.
In water it was silver, covert, still.

Reaching the black feather
of the tree-line, it was caught,
paused, a silhouette of light

we held to as a window
left uncurtained to bring in dawn
after a long night.

That labour under an anchor
of wings, that quality of weight,
we named grace honed to the sky,

let it leave us for its own element –
breaking into a blind of cloud
waiting low to catch it –

thought nothing more of until,
later that day, a signal against purity,
a flash on cloth, blood came.

Miscarriage

On the scan you saw a heart beat
within a curl of new flesh.
I saw that couched ball of life
as a windfallen and bitten apple
already decaying among the leaves.

So you had proof of existence,
believed at once our child would live.
I had a week bleeding painful roses,
proof that what is grown on faith
becomes the space it leaves.

We returned to await death's angel.
It came from the window at midnight,
dropped black wings about the bed
where I laboured. We knew that moment's loss
under its encasing fist.

We abandoned each other to sadness,
what we carried and could not speak,
to filling in days with our hands
wondering where all the holes have come from
sprouting like fungi among the dead trees.

To The Spider

We have broken the web
you wove across our door.
Each night we gazed at you,

the fat humbug of your belly
swinging at the gathered centre,
a lamp hanging under the moon.

We have been careless,
a grain of anger in us breaking through
what you must make and remake,

forgetting you in favour of ourselves.
And so you have left us,
fingering torn threads in the dark.

Suddenly

There are no more poems.
It does not follow that tomorrow will follow.
Your strong arm resting against your book
may say one thing,
but I am unable to know you right now.

The evenings lengthen under electricity,
drawn out by boredom, or is it compliance?
We break black chocolate
into tiny pieces, pass
them to each other's waiting mouths.

Stories filter through us their various lights
until we are opaque, multicoloured
yet no wiser. Locked
beneath our separate findings
our shared fragments dissolve unheard.

The cat flits between our hands,
hoping for a hint of wildness, or love –
that abandoned fellowship.
Something of us bleeds away.
Make us stronger, more pure in the vein.

East

There has been no rain all spring,
the river is drowning in a stream of mud.
In the current of my blood, life is poised;
I push down to reach it.

June is thunder and downpour.
Poppies scatter their silks in blowsy,
overgrown gardens. We thank the bruised
horizon, make love to the rain in us.

At the solstice we head for the sea.
We are alone, except for the woman
with her field-glasses trained
one long, shocking moment upon us.

At the flush of tide our new child
shows itself, a coil of red light
discovered at the ocean bed, now held
between our salt-wet minds.

After the storm we find sea-jewels,
a shore necklace loosed and scattered
at the tide's edge, one electric vein
running through the crystal flesh.

They are the water's gifts; the tide
will return to claim them. We gaze,
hold them like a broken wing
or the head of a violet,

while at the centre of each palm
they leave a flushed bruise
where their gentle sting has entered.

Fruit

We crushed cherries, raspberries, strawberries,
all the red fruits our bed could hold.
The sheets ran with their juice,
their bruised skins puckering and splitting,
darkening against us.

This is our bounty, I whispered, holding
your head to my nipple. I wanted
to enter you, my milk coming.
Pressing my hips wide you entered me:
slow, hard, surprising.

On the balcony the sun raged,
palms lifted exotic skirts. Below, a garden
grew its fruits in hectic beds.
Together we fingered them, grasped
at the roots to feel the water swelling there.

To An Unborn

You grew inside me
and now I will worship you,
if, for thirty days and thirty nights
you wait, completed,
a love poem folded
between the leaves of my book.

Lay up fat, store visions.
You must not arrive before your time.
Your skull insists
where my bone softens
and I touch finger to your finger
running the gauntlet inside.

I am preparing our bed,
the silken cottons for your earth-skin.
The house is tipped
out and put back again.
The birth room hangs
between Lavender and Mozart.

Into my dreaming you extend
a hand, egg-blue and pulsing.
Each finger is capped
with a soft white nail.
You tap in a language I read
with my eyes shut.

Is this a moon-month
we are stealing? Its silver disk
slips over my tongue.
These days I feel
the light touch through
my newly cracked skin.

I will unravel it, now a skein
like the cloud rushed sky,
make you an armour,
little warrior. With this
you may draw near, enter
the world's fierce gate.

Riding The Waves To Bring You Home

These horses wreck themselves on the black shore,
hammer their limbs at the sea gates.
I cut my body on scarred muscle,
at my waist your anchor rope.

My voice is taken in anger, this recklessness;
I cast bloody scraps to haul you in.
These hooves are un-ironed, and native,
slice like rock into bone

as your head crowns in my hands,
its sodden pelt in salted waves
exposing the scalp – its shelf, well, pulse.

Harvest

They have cut the corn
the colour of his hair.
The fields lie exhausted with it, lovesick.

The sun lives now under his skin.
I warm myself by it,
and his womb face when we wake to suckle.

Forgive me this, but his mouth
is the sweetest, ripest strawberry,
tempting, tempting,

and I cannot keep my hands
from the black furze
that hackles his salmon back.

One day it will darken, his hair,
to the nut brown of eyes
already reflecting rubies,

those eyes, birthed these nine months
from their milky husks,
ripened, like mine, from dark kernels.

My Son The Horse

I dreamt my son had become a horse.
I was his red mother ,
it showed in his hair and in his eye,
a fire leaping up inside.

He ran with me, tugging
at the training bit. His shoulder
was lining with new muscle,
his feathered foot cut the earth.

In his heart swelled a river.
He grew a hand daily
and the black of his father bloomed
a hide of dark roses.

In three years I will break him.
We will ride the high hill.
What power we will own
when his broad back strengthens.

Lugh And The Light

1. First Light

On your first morning your eyes held the blue
filtering through the small high window
as if they had kept, just for this moment,
their nine month's vigil in the opalescent womb.

We had not slept, and would not for days yet.
You were all there was, you who had entered
here to bring the night to a standstill,
the morning quietly bowing to its knees.

And months later, this was your first word:
Light! Light! And we all looked up, amazed
as you reached for the fluorescent sky,

unwrapped the parcel of sounds gilded
in the cocoon of your apprenticeship,
set them loose to dry their brilliant wings.

2. Night Lights

You command the sun back to bed,
would have the moon again.
splendid in her twilight velvets.

You woke once shouting her name;
through the curtains her cool face
looked in, come to soothe your fever.

I had to turn you away from her,
fold my own love into your open arms,
the cold back of my hand on your cheek.

Nightly, you press your body to the glass,
point out the pole star, an aeroplane
winking across the sky.

Your fingers imitate the flickering
sign of your song, its mantra condensing
to a cloud of breath rings.

Great Bear hangs in the window's frame,
poised in his winter aspect
as on the eve of your birth.

He has captured the crescent lantern
and keeps it for his heart;
his lady stamps her brightness on the dark.

3. Light Maker

Water flutters from your hand.
The hose held high, its light
fragments over your face.

Wings halo, absorb you,
pale butterflies ignite
then dissolve at your feet.

You delight in the shower.
Your belly is a glass pot
that pouts and shines with wine,

and, of course, your blond head
is back-lit: you are crowned,
a little plumed bird.

I want never to forget this,
but know that each moment
is eclipsed by the next;

then you stumble, fall,
my sun-blind eyes fix
you in amber, a burning star.

Wish!

The canal wears a coat of blossom,
pink heads flock densely on the still water;
it is muggy, before storm weather.

A mouth bubbles the surface.
My *Fish!* becomes your *Wish!*
The rippled skin is bright with captured sun.

I could allow for a moment
the light gathered at the apex of petals
to hold out its candy promises,

but in the weedy depths the dark flexes,
forms itself into something muscular,
advances on the bank where we stand,

me gripping your too small, ungraspable
hand as you sway towards the edge,
the dropped posy of closing flowers.

Starfish

Asleep you are a starfish,
your skin is submarine, your charged element.
You are skating, each finger
a water pearl balanced beneath the surface.

This is how I leave you,
suspended in the blue aria of your dream.
Like this my love floods in
and I could drown here, the sea filling my mouth.

Only unwatched can I release
this close harboured pain. I see light descend
through the water's cavern,
rain gently on your stippled belly.

Waiting as you dive for ocean bed,
your dark abyss, I keep the boat steady.
You are too deep to call back,
your eyes shells, your soul a luminous tail.

May Angel

His cock stood past his hip,
his beast's foot tip-toed the hill,
one vast cirrus wing reached behind him,
the other saluted a poppy blue sky.

I left our sleeping child, came
to where you sat, face to the window.
All the clouds were cold breaths
and like old dreams had lost their meaning.

I wanted to bring you what I had seen,
and the beauty of our child's mouth,
his rice-paper lids, the day's light in them,
the fat gift of his hand on my face,

but I could not speak. Instead I listened
as you detailed the wisps of a beard
you could have curled on your tongue
and the pole star igniting in a satyr's eye.

At The Dead Sea Shore

We wake in the blue midnight.
At our feet your waters roll
and unroll in their deceptive flight.
We had thought you still,
sunken, as you are, in the planet's crust,
such a distillation of millennial
dust, you are weighted in its overcoat.
Carelessly we laid our sheets
at your shore to overhear the boat
of the dreaming sea talking,
as we fancied you would in your long sleep.
But you are walking,
riding the dark passage of the night
between the nations who stamp
at your banks. The moon is at its height,
dragging the water into its net,
and us with it. We are consumed by a wave,
spat out again onto the mud, wet,
delirious with fear and convinced
you have risen to reclaim your lands,
(for even you are shrinking, blitzed
by five billion daily exhalations)
your deserts, your cities, your mountains.

Shooting the Palestinian

The melon fields purpled
under the setting sun's hammer.
I believe they led to Jerusalem.

We squatted on the rise of a hill,
the gourds' swollen backs
hunched in rows to the horizon.

We smoked the Lebanese hash,
drawing fire to our faces;
a sentry stamped in the black distance.

Later we hacked the green hide
along its pink lines, sliced
the crisp flesh into vats of vodka,

and sucking the saturated fruit
recounted minor acts of violence:
how an old blind dog refused to die,

dragging its entrails to the river
before drowning; how I spent a night
slicing giant cockroaches

into shiny slivers, their metal legs
still scrabbling at the lino,
until, defeated, I learned to live with them.

Czech Pieces

For Olga Steinerova

1. River Music

In Prague I played Dvořák
and all the birds answered,
casting themselves in sound.

The notes were water on glass
breaking against its surface;
the harmony built on air

until I threw open the window
and could not distinguish
between the given and the received.

My soul became a blown egg,
its inner skin coming away
like formed milk on my hands.

The music was throwing this,
its net webbing the afternoon light,
a kaleidoscope on the wall;

and the wings breaking rhythm
in my chest, scattering there,
weaving me through with new bone.

2. Wild Boar in Šarka

At four a.m. the streets were liberated
by the first snow. Half-cut, we tipped
from the bar on Staré-Město, stepped
into a moony dream, a black city glistening.

We were walking home to the outskirts,
Šarka Valley, where the city unravelled
to a struggle of brown fields and farmhouses,
now a village under glass in a snowstorm.

The saints on Karlův Most wore hooded shawls
of sugared lace, dropped iced almonds
from frozen hands as we passed – Christmas
coming again in February – only this time truer.

At Šarka the mouth of the valley was lit
with frost forming on the silvered drifts
and we remembered the boar that stopped a girl
last week, stamped, snorted, shot flames

at her crotch, scattered to the dark wood
where we now stood on the steep path,
snared by the crisp patter of cloven prints,
the breathy bulk steaming in the night.

3. The Bridge

We passed out of the city
to where your parents, after the war,
built their weekend cottage
on the slopes above the peasant river.

It was late autumn. The wind's
tongue hardened on our faces
as we tasted the iron of the season
in a handful of berries.

On the bridge we looked down
to water furious between our feet
and in the white rush of sound
woke into the dark

where your mother listened
to the man on the radio,
fear unravelling its thread in her hands,
and your father held you

in the wings of the quilt,
the tremor in his chest
a butterfly against your cheek.
In 1968 you were five years old.

You spoke only your native language
around which your tongue
slipped, freeing its subtleties,
but heard then as we hear now

the stamp of boots on metal
as an army crossed the bridge,
tanks, like driven beasts,
crushing stones in the road.

4. Windfalls

Your neighbour offered his fallen apples,
the orchard thick with them after a sudden frost.
We filled plastic bags with the rosy bulbs,
left a squelching nest of bruises around each tree.

We ate fistfuls all day, their sweet cold juice
on our lips and fingers; baked a bowlful
stuffed with raisins and cinnamon sugar
for supper, drenched in cream the steamy flesh.

In the morning you woke me, naked and alert.
I had to join you, undressing at the pump
in the ice hard yard, shouting out to trees and river
the imperative of water chilled underground.

At breakfast your neighbour came, laughing.
He had seen us, aeroplaning like his two boys,
ecstatic in our skins. *Sblka*, he mouthed, and together
                                                    we cut
segments of fruit, the sap of apple rising from the knife.

*Sblka: apple

5. Eclipse

The child brought us fire,
a clasp of grasses breathed awake
through his smoking hands.
We warmed ourselves.

The lake was tarnished,
rubbed of colour. It crouched
there, on the edge of winter.
Our tongues lapped the pool of sky.

We women were the cup,
the child an egg nestled within us,
We watched him launch a ship
of leaves and spent feathers.

Heading home, he took flight,
harboured, high up, on a branch.
We called and called, held
our faces flat to the sunken light;

heard then the tone of ourselves
set ringing with the plunge
and resonance of a stone on water,
under a bleached-out curtain of sky

where the forked sun hung,
a sickle hammered
from the metal of the moon.

6. The Mushroom Pickers

At dawn we left the house,
gloves, a basket, a sleepy dream
under our arms, an oat biscuit
passed around, stepped into a halo
of mist and disappeared

to re-emerge in the forest,
great black wet trunks rising
in battalion into far away sky.
We bent amongst the dew-
soaked ferns, unravelling

the tight curled tendrils
just to exclaim how the first artist
used this blueprint to scratch
her mark in stone. But mushrooms
were the gold we sifted

for, shining and sticky
from their overnight births,
clustered in a hollow or alone
amongst the leaf debris and bracken,
unable to hide the insistence

of living, if only for a morning.

7. On The Train To Ceské Krumlov

Bohemia dressed in frost, her earth feet
shimmering in crystal slippers,
touched her white toes to the tracks
as we rattled across her southern skirts.

We swayed to the narrow gauge lullaby,
drawing our black lines behind us
as if scoring out the pain of months in the city,
a bird trailing broken feathers in the snow.

Where were we headed? I see a river
arrested by ice en route through a tiny
sugar-almond town; tucked into the hill
two bears turn in their brown coats.

We might uncover our love, swimming
forcefully under the frozen river, if only
we could reach its embrace, hold
our hands to warm flowers in the ice.

But in my memory we are always travelling.
I stand at a window drawing breath,
the exhaled cold of this winter land
burns its death's light in my chest.

In her castle on the hill our love waits,
sucking the bones of loneliness,
while, crouched in dreaming minds, the town
guards the primal blood at her heart.

8. Into The City

Four years have passed since with you I first
crossed this river. In daytime the bridge lines
with watercolours and violinists;
now midnight has swept its paving clean.

And this time we battle, our positions entrenched
with each poised step, each turn and gesture,
yours more Wild West than West, mine a crumbling
East turning Eastern out of the ruins.

Until this: a man knelt on cardboard
under a lantern-wielding saint. He rocks,
a mourner at the wall, hands clasped,
incanting; it is to us he is praying.

His prayer is made of hunger, one blackened
bitten down hand a stub without fingers.
What we offer him is anger: at Capitalism,
at man's failure. It does not matter.

I throw coins, you the toe of your boot.
We both continue on our way.

Fold

For Pauline

The sheep have left their cold selves
where fields touch white at the snow line.
We have huddled them to the fold,
the *Prima Maters*, and, counting them
into the scented dark, hold for a second
each nubbed head, each startled mouth:
become women now, preparing to birth.

And women too, we slip to talk
of our own labours, come close
like the folding in of the sea,
a caul of water tightening at our chests.
Our children sleep in the house, guarded
by fathers, but arrive on night's taut cord
as each hot flank heaves.

I watch you deliver the first,
a big, black-legged boy you pull
by the hoof and nose, stretching the ewe,
her giving sex opening in one last flood
of relief and fluid. We rub the warm
back into the lamb, the breath
in our mouths metal with womb-blood.

At this distance the tug is brutal,
a twitch on the fragile skin
of unhealed memory, all our birth's wounds.

Spook

I mistake a cow for a woman,
a sack of darkness, a black jacket
broad shouldering the horizon,
and I think – she waits for me
to answer her slow coming.

She has been gathering flesh
for weeks, rising out of the dip
in the field each time I look,
her white face filling the window
with wide-drawn eyes.

And here, where hazel have grown
to full height in a group, a coven,
a whispering hive, I'm sure
she balanced her handful of lights
on the wind between the leaves.

Wind

The wind was a great crow
beating her wings, a savage old bitch.
I lay beneath her, the air
black smoke, its noise in my throat
a catch of stones.

The barn mooned, not a boat
at sea, but a cave within a waking mountain;
and this was no storm,
but the laboured breath of an angry hag
who'd climbed the hill.

Whether I woke or dreamt
stillness fell like masked oxygen.
I was calmed, my head held
by night's hand in night's lap,
her skirts warming my shoulders,

while outside on the cobbled yard
clogs pattered: apples falling
into a basket, soft rain coming
to cleanse eyes and mouths
after bringing in the harvest.

Birch In Winter

What stops me is the explosion
of limbs, almost white,
and closer, a pearl of rain
reflecting the green hill.

Below, water chants its dream
over rocks and a crow
drops quietly out of the sky,
picks amongst the leaves.

It takes off at the sight of me
leaving behind its cry –
a stone falling
cold and compact as thunder.

Then, is it because for a moment
I am lost, and rub
my hand along a branch,
or simply the fact of turning away,

but coming back to that tree
clasped to the wet bank,
the light has changed
to dark now not silver,

the nibbled bark
no longer rings with the glitter
of raindrops, but lies
emptied out, haggard,

and I hear again the wind
throw itself over the hill,
the day retreating
before the onslaught of night.

Cornwall 1974

Love is an ocean I cannot forget...
David Byrne – Talking Heads

My father dreams of drowning at the shore,
tidal waves of boats, fish big as houses.
It is always night and thundering.

I am with him yet not with him. I lie
hiding in the jaws of a shark, fretting
for a little girl stolen by the tide.

And all the time the sea rolled inwards
he was watching me, gleaning
a rock pool for a pebble of quartz,

the breath of the ocean cold on my back,
sudden cloud a stranger imminent
with loss. But only now do I see

my father reaching out both hands,
the cigarette falling from his mouth
as he calls, winds in the invisible line,

draws me across the precarious divide –
an enchanted beast dipping
out of my own element into his.

When I Was Young

I tried to conjure a husband
from a box of bits kept under the bed:
a twist of hair in a shiny clip,

three blue beads on a broken twine.
For a moment he was there, his eyes
turned to me, surprised to be alive.

In a cache of time, a velvet pouch
that once held a signature ring,
tiny, for the little finger,

I am kneeling to a child.
It is autumn, a park, the trees a gold embrace.
We run in circles, kicking up leaves.

The future is like this: a movie
on old grain I cannot put words to,
an unfamiliar memory my father

might offer me while we sit
with coffee in our hands in a cafe
on the edge of the woods;

treasures I gather in the shoebox,
what I love and cannot leave.
Their potencies thrill beneath the lid.

Passage

I stood at the kitchen table,
between my legs the fat wedge of a towel.
I smelt of old metal, the sea,
a ship leaking its dangerous cargo.

You were at the sink, and at my words,
I've started, you turned, leant
to light a cigarette from the gas ring.
The distance between us was unfathomable.

Last night my body rolled its tidal wave,
swept away land, cows, a whole village;
in its place was a bloody pool
where small hands waved for help.

You looked at me. It was like raining
inside a window we could touch,
smell, that drenched us the moment
we thought ourselves safe;

and then, smoke curling into your hair,
misting the light, you turned away,
embraced the incurable need to step
outside, watch the rain soak in.

The Night Before Your Funeral

I made love to my husband
in a stranger's bed, felt the sorrow balloon
in my mouth, which I refused to open.
My unborn was wakeful; he turned and kicked,
weighed heavily upon me.

I took the dream as a sign. *Release me*,
you said. Your face was a mask
of worry and sadness.
You were at the chapel window
restless for the wings you had been promised.

I had not seen you for a year.
I could imagine you beachcombing
or sketching the roots of a tree,
sunlight shattering through leaves,
your hands a mosaic

and I wanted most to touch your hands,
your muscular hands edgy
with life, your father's hands trembling
as you reached in the dark
for my sleeping face.

But a glacier was moving
through me, settling its stones.
I had become earth. My eyes
darkened with silt and I heard only
the tapping of water far away,

the fact of your emaciated
body, your bird's chest cracked
open on the marble, the bruise
that must mean you now wear your heart
black, on the outside.

Sculpture, Girl Standing

I believe I know why you bought her.
The date, 1976, is marked on her foot.
Proof, that we did, you and I, hand
in hand, run along the pavement in the rain
to the shop where she waited for us,
our stone child, our little keepsake.
Proof that we stood in the gallery
steaming and stamping and excited
as you handed over seventy pounds.
I remember. Yes, I remember.

And why, in my dream last night
I saw your death's face as this child's:
the fat, full cheeks, the hair curled
tightly at your temple, the rich mouth
opening its lips, about to speak,
and why your proud belly revealed
its salmon's pink serrated flesh
as I slid my fearful hand
into cleansed and gutted meat, heard:
It is nothing. This is my earth skin. Eat.

Aknowledgements

Acknowledgements are due to the Editors of the following magazines and anthologies where some of these poems first appeared: *New Welsh Review Poetry Ireland, Poetry Wales, Poetry London, The Rialto, Take Twenty, Reactions, Oxygen* (Seren).

'The Kitchen God' was first published in *The Ring of Words, The Arvon/Telegraph Poetry Competition Anthology*, 1998.

I would like to offer love and thanks to my husband Ruari Martin for his unfailing support during the writing of this book; also Gabrielle Russell and Jess Penrose for their friendship and wisdom.